MARY LOUISE SHELTON

MARY LOUISE SHELTON

Silence Isn't Golden

A Journey to Healing

Mary Louise Shelton

MARY LOUISE SHELTON

The man who murdered my brother will not be dignified with a name,
real or fiction. I refer to him only as 'MBM' (My Brother's Murderer).

Likewise, the man who repeatedly raped my mother will be referred
to only as 'JDR' (John Doe Rapist).

PREFACE

Giving up the hope that the past could be any different and letting go, so that it does not hold you hostage, and accepting what has happened, knowing you cannot change what is done...

— *Oprah Winfrey*

These are difficult things to reconcile when you have been the victim of abuse.

Learning to love yourself and knowing that you are worthy of love and deserve compassion can be illusive realizations. Healing is continual and takes a lifetime of commitment.

Speak up and speak out to let others know you need help and they will help you. Ease the pain and smooth the path for those who share your journey and together you will walk out of darkness and into light.

Silence Isn't golden.

Darkness cannot drive out darkness: only light can do that. Hate cannot drive out hate: only love can do that.

— *Martin Luther King, Jr.*

DEDICATION

Silence Isn't Golden is dedicated to those from whom I have taken inspiration and who have given me the courage to seek the light of a new day.

And to all who suffer in silence, this book is dedicated to you.

I also dedicate this book in memory of Esther Tate, a stranger, who gave me hope and support while assisting me at my lowest point when I was homeless after a car wreck. It was an honor to know her as she was an absolute angel. Abundant Life Ministries in Chapel Hill, NC, which she started, still offers hope to those in need, in her name.

This book is also dedicated to the memory of Reverend Virginia Wyatt, a friend and minister during the trials and tribulations with my struggles to get back on my feet.

And to Nancy King, a member of my writer's group, I further dedicate this book. Nancy's offer to assist me came at a time when I needed it most, to allow me to fulfill a dream and reach out to those who need a voice. Typing and editing my manuscript is an answer to a prayer. I am so eternally grateful.

CONTENTS

CHAPTER 1

A Dark Beginning

Each of us is a book waiting to be written, and that book, if written, results in a person explained.

— Thomas M. Cirignano

Almost seven decades ago, a beautiful girl made her debut – screaming – into the world!

Following a lengthy labor, I cried relentlessly, but my exhausted mother could not hear me. The third child born to two hearing-impaired parents, I was named for my paternal grandmother, Mary Louise.

My brother Charles, was two years older than myself. My oldest brother, Henry, had been snatched from the hospital at birth.

Mother's hospital roommate told her that Henry was taken because he was a bi-racial baby and that she should not have any more babies at that institution.

"You're deaf and dumb. Go home and have another one! But don't come back to this hospital."

What rights were they going to exert in that day and time as a bi-racial deaf-mute couple trying to work and earn a living? They had to survive in an uncaring world.

The sorrow and burden of Henry's disappearance must have been overwhelming. I don't recall them talking about it much. Their pain was buried in silence. We never saw him again. The mystery of his kidnapping haunts me every day. I am still looking for Henry.

I wanted so very much to reunite Henry and Mother for her 100th birthday that I hired a private detective to look for my brother, but to no avail. There were seven male babies born on the same day, September 7, 1944, in that hospital, so locating Henry seemed like a possibility. It was not to be.

My parents had met and fallen in love at a school for the deaf in Raleigh, North Carolina, where because they were an inter-racial couple, they could not marry legally.

It was hard in the south to fit in. They were different as a couple; my mother was black, my father was white, and neither could hear nor speak.

Lillie and Lewis, prior to marriage

So, they moved north to Detroit, Michigan in search of a more accepting environment to marry and start a family. I spent my early years in Detroit.

It was while there on Hendricks Street that my innocence was taken, and my life changed forever.

My Uncle Claude, the brother of my mother, repeatedly took advantage of me, an innocent babe in my crib, which continued until we moved to another house in Detroit several years later.

At the new location, my dad rented out a room to a distant cousin, a deaf boxer, who repeatedly raped my mom while Dad was at work. By now, a pre-teen, I was the one who had to go and make out police reports for my mom, who did not want my dad to know. It was part of a series of events that would become a ritual of, 'cannot tell Dad what happened.'

I don't remember why the responsibility fell to me instead of my brother, or why Charles didn't respond to Mother's constant yelling and crying from the rapes. Even though his room was upstairs - surely he heard the excruciating sounds coming from her room, too many times to count, but as usual it fell on me to wait until it was over and go with her to file the police reports.

Being a CODA (Child of Deaf Adults) comes with lots of responsibilities and many related difficulties. The Deaf Culture in which I grew up was a silent one and because of that, an isolated one. My parents did not trust the 'hearing world' because they did not 'belong' to it. As a result, they were very strict about not participating in it and ran a dictatorship in which my brother and I were to be seen and not heard.

My controlled environment included females doing all the inside chores, and males doing all the outside chores. This was before perma-press, so I had to iron everything that went through the washing machine including sheets, towels, and the work clothes my dad wore every day in a manufacturing plant.

Our meals were just as regimented and never varied. We ate cabbage every Monday, greens on Tuesday, string beans on Wednesday, etc. I don't know if our monotonous diet had anything to do with it, but I never missed a day of school and like my parents, was never sick – no colds, flu, or anything else. However, I do not eat cabbage to this day!

Furthermore, my brother and I were not allowed to mingle with children from 'divorced households' which meant I only had one playmate, Evette, who lived across the street. I could play with Evette because she was in a two-parent home. Evette had two younger sisters. She was my age. We walked to school together and shared many happy hours. In fact, we remain in contact today. She has been one of the constants in my life, one of the strings that holds my past and present together – the bad and the good. She has known me through it all.

My family had one television, but my brother, who was my mom's favorite, would sabotage my programs to get Mother to watch his 'Cowboy and Indian' shows rather than "I Love Lucy". He tricked her into thinking that it was a 'sexually' related show because of the word *Love* in the title, instead of a comedy. She never watched television other than Dragnet or Perry Mason until she was in her eighties.

Unlike most children, I never went to the beach, never went to restaurants, went to movies maybe twice, and little else.

I took clarinet in school; loved it, so Mom hated it. She beat me every day, so my brother Charles took me to the police station one day and asked if they could take me to a foster home.

They said, "no," explaining that, "she will live through the beatings, she will NOT live through the rapes that occur in foster care."

In the end, I was glad the policemen did not remove me from my home because my uncle disappeared and the sexual assaults on me stopped. However, they continued on my mom well into my teens.

My memories of my childhood as a whole are mostly blocked out.

In later years, I struggled with chronic depression. I sought help of psychotherapists and psychiatrists, but for reasons I've never understood, they did not want to discuss my past.

Whenever I wanted to bring up my old wounds, they would pass it off saying: "We need to deal with the here and now.

Why are you depressed today?

What brings you here now?

Why do you hate your job and have road rage?

Why do you have anger and weight issues now?"

Well, all the guilt and shame from my mother's brother molesting me and the fact that I got no support from my mom, probably had a lot to do with it. Burying all that for so many years was a horrible burden. I ended up unable to love myself, because

I could not get love and support in my own household.

I had no voice and no one to stop it.

No one to hear me. No one to care.

My mother was the only one in her family who was born deaf and mute. So, her attitude was one of blind acceptance – such things happen.

What happened to me was something to just cover up and deal with by "not telling." That is what was taught to her. If it is family – you do not tell.

If any of this sounds familiar, remember you do have choices. You do have a voice. There are alternatives. There is now support. # me too -- # times up There are support groups and hot lines. Use them!

Since it was her brother that molested me, we could not tell. I grew up feeling abandoned and unloved and unsupported.

I didn't believe I was worthy of love. *So, how do I look in the mirror and feel loved?*

That's how the process of looking outside oneself for love starts. That's how children without voices begin to act out and make bad decisions such as weight gain, relationship choices, drugs, etc.

CHAPTER 2

The Long Arm of Fear

Children should be carefree, playing in the sun; not living a nightmare in the darkness of the soul.

— *Dave Pelzer*

It was a lazy Sunday afternoon and I had settled comfortably in front of the television, with a cup of coffee, to watch an episode of Oprah. She was interviewing William Young, author of "The Shack". Young was talking about relationships; relationships with people and relationships with God. He opined on the meaning of love, saying, "If love is forced, it is no love at all." He spoke openly about having an affair and his wife confronting him with the news that "she knew." It was a compelling interview.

Then, Oprah asked him this; what I find to be a most difficult question – *what was it like being a child?*

I find that question so hard, because I don't really know what it's like. Most of my childhood is blocked out. I know I was molested. I know little else.

Growing Up

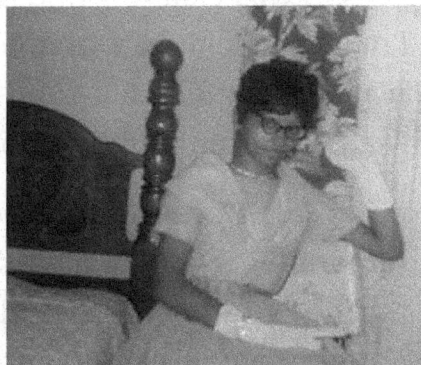

Mary Jones
Mary and Junior, upper right

Young, also confided to Oprah and to the world in that moment that he had been molested as a child.

I sat up and listened more intently.

I could really relate. I could identify with this man on my television screen. He is the author of a best-selling book and a successful movie, with thoughts and feelings just like mine. And he sees God as a black-skinned woman! We had much in common.

As a child lying helplessly alone, I can remember *him*. He had come to my crib; what should have been my sanctuary, my place of rest and peace. He was a one-armed black man. That's what I remember. What I don't remember is my *childhood*.

I was violated, and my childhood was destroyed. I may have played with marbles here and there or played a game of hide and seek, but mostly it's a blank. *No*, I don't remember enjoying my childhood at all.

I don't remember movies, or friends. I don't remember school teachers. I can't recall a class or a teacher's name. I can recall a Latin teacher's face, but not her name. I remember taking the bus and getting good grades. I was not allowed to participate in school activities outside of classes, so my only joy was playing the clarinet.

My mother thought musicians were low life drug dealers so she wouldn't let me play music at home, even though we lived next door to a world renowned jazz musician, Charlie Gabriel. Oh, how I wanted my own clarinet and to have Charlie Gabriel tutor me. I got slapped for even saying, "hello" to my neighbor, who happened to be happily married to a beautiful woman, ironically named Mary.

Charles was allowed to go to the Gabriel's to learn to play chess. I envied all the people I have encountered who talk about wonderful childhoods. I wasn't even allowed to visit my dad at his workplace because of his race. His co-workers never knew he was married to a black woman. We lived a regimented life of church and school; fun was not in the equation.

I don't remember anyone ever coming to my rescue or anything like that. I've blocked it out! My memories have been affected by severe trauma as a baby. I remember the one-armed molester.

My mother had a "so what" mentality, probably because she was raped, causing her to have fear throughout her life. She relied on me to file police reports and not say anything to my dad. My turmoil throughout life stems a lot from that, I'm sure. I don't know why she didn't run or want anything done or want anyone to know; but she wanted to file reports!

The boxer who rented the room was at least twenty years younger than her, but stronger and more powerful. Perhaps we needed the income from his rent. She was deaf and mute, and weaker. For many reasons, I will never understand, my mother endured and held on to her secret, our secret. But, silence isn't golden.

Many years have passed. My mother and I reached a level of reconciliation later in life. It's the only thing we knew to do, to try and make some sense of it all. Mother is gone now, but the feelings remain. I know others share them, too. Like I identified with William Young from a television interview, there are others out there who have stories like mine and must be heard!

In reaching out to others, I've served as an interpreter for the hearing impaired. George, a fellow interpreter and caretaker for a teenage girl whom I'll call Carla, has a story. Carla lived in fear - fear because she did not believe deaf people would live long.

So, for reassurance, she asked to speak with my mother by videophone, as my deaf mother had lived a long life. I made those arrangements and I know both benefited from the conversation.

Carla was raped by her mother's boyfriends, repeatedly. Her mother took away the social media account on her phone to prevent her from going out and giving herself sexually to men on the street that she'd contacted via the Internet.

Carla had no guidelines for sex. No one stopped the mother's boyfriends. No one responded to Carla's disguised pleas for help. No one seemed to care. But, silence isn't golden.

Such atrocities are certainly not limited to children who are deaf. I imagine it happens in the hearing world too, where daughters are living at home with mothers that just choose their boyfriends over their daughters.

My mother happened to be deaf, and her mother happened to be hearing. Abuse and rape and negligence occur in families everywhere, to innocent children and adults, each with a story to be heard.

Although you may be afraid to tell someone because you fear the consequences, speaking up and speaking out will be the first step to healing. The physical abuse must stop so you can begin to deal with the trauma and heal your soul. A law enforcement officer, a social worker or counselor, a friend or a

parent; someone will listen and help you.

CHAPTER 3

Junior

Innocence, once lost, can never be regained.
Darkness, once gazed upon, can never be lost.

— John Milton

I miss my brother. We'd been through a lot together, and there was much life ahead of us waiting to be shared. But Junior was murdered, and it was pure chaos that followed. My daughter acted out. My father grieved and wanted to die. My brother, Charles assumed his identity. It's not that he took over his name or used his credit cards; it was more like he tried to get close to him in bizarre ways. Junior's favorite color was blue, so Charles would wear only blue. And me? I was angry. The task of dealing with the funeral arrangements fell to me.

At twenty-seven years of age, I assumed the role of a parent and an administrator. I took over and did my best. I couldn't understand how my brother could be alive and well one day and dead the next. The police inquiries and the private detectives – all trying to understand what had happened, and why. Who was the killer?

The answer turned out to be a man named MBM, the brother of the woman who was pregnant with Junior's child.

Junior was attending college in Ypsilanti when he got a girl pregnant and refused to marry her. The girl's brother seemed to take issue with the fact that Junior wanted to be a playboy and not a father. In his rage over the pregnancy, he shot and killed my brother; a cold and senseless act I can never reconcile in my mind. Why? To what purpose? My dear brother gone in an instant.

Lewis Palmer Jones, Jr.

Junior was found with his hands tied behind his back and shot 6 times in the head! Jr's blood was on MBM's clothes, but that was before DNA testing and I was told that all the evidence was circumstantial.

I read several letters from Junior to this girl explaining that in his observation of my marriage, and Charles's marriage, that marriage was out of the question! Junior said there would be no *Shot Gun Wedding* - he did not have a job and was not going to get a job. Junior never worked a day in his life and he had no plans to support himself, let alone a baby.

MBM drove a fancy Cadillac and Junior asked to drive it. The car was found where Junior was found.

A friend of Jr's asked me point blank, "Do you want me to shoot him?" I replied, "I can't tell you to do that. I have a conscience." She did it anyway, shot him three times. He survived and as far as I know he was never arrested for the crime.

I was so consumed with his murder and wanting to participate in getting something done legally, I hired a Private Investigator. The fact that there was blood on MBM's clothes, that MBM's car was right there and Junior had asked for permission to drive it and the fact that MBM was at my parent's house and used them for an alibi – all added up to compelling evidence, but the police did not agree. "No gun, no witness, no crime!" To be told by the Police Department that I watch too much TV and that all the evidence was circumstantial was too much for me to hear!

I was informed by the Private Investigator in our last conversation that MBM was arrested on drug charges in North Carolina. The possibility of him talking about it in jail was a long-shot and continuing to pursue that path, would consume time and money that I didn't have. I have refused to be part of any jury since his death because I do not believe justice was served by the Detroit Police Department in pursuit of Jr's killer.

MBM may have been locked up for drug charges, but I guess he got away with murder.

Junior made some bad choices. He lived life on the edge. Like me, he had demons that he could not shake. He deserved better. I lost my innocence, Junior lost his life.

I cannot understand. I *can* forgive. Some things are just too evil to contemplate and defy all attempts at human reason. But, if I cannot forgive, I cannot be forgiven.

CHAPTER 4

An Angel Amongst Us

I could not have made it this far had there not been angels along the way.

— Della Reese

I don't remember exactly how the car accident happened, but I ended up in the hospital in Greensboro, North Carolina. I'd recently moved from California and taken a job as a nanny caring for the newborn baby of a physician and her lawyer husband in the college town of Chapel Hill. I wanted to work again as a social worker and figured I'd take the nanny job until I could make that happen.

Free room and board and a salary – just a little more time; it was all going to work out for me. I just needed my records with my social worker credentials in order to be employed in North Carolina. But I was dealt a ferocious double blow when the couple fired and evicted me while I lay in my hospital bed recovering from my injuries. "You no longer have a place to stay. We have to have a nanny and you're not it," the woman said coldly at my bedside. I thought to myself, "*This* is considered Southern hospitality?"

I didn't have children with me, and as a single adult, a shelter was my only option.

My fee would be paid for one night. I don't know how it happened, but for some reason I was united with the kind-hearted Esther Tate and her Abundant Life Boarding House in Chapel Hill. She was known around town as a Good Samaritan who sought out homeless women, finding them on the street and bringing them to her facility.

I was one of those lucky women. She took me in and said she'd help me because I needed a lot of medical care. Miss Tate did this on the premise that I would pay her back the $50 a week for board and care.

Food and laundry facilities were available on the main floor. On the second floor were rooms and TVs and space for personal belongings for the women residents. Each woman had her own room. Miss Tate welcomed me without knowing who I was, and that meant the world to me.

Meanwhile, I'd been talking with my mom trying to get her to set me up while my social worker records were being located in California. No one could find my records. It was as though I hadn't even been a social worker in Van Nuys. Evidence of my qualifications were just lost in some kind of a hole.

I was feeling hopeless. Miss Tate introduced me to a Christian lady Virginia, who became a dear friend.

I worked at a local grocery store as a cashier and as a nurse's aide, a horrible job that I hated because I disliked changing grown men's diapers, but was able to save enough money to make good on the agreement with Miss Tate. For that, she really commended me as being one of the very few that actually paid her back. I stayed at Miss Tate's boarding house for six months. I will always cherish the kindness from her.

My mother had told me to go back to California – back where I came from. She was not going to assist me. I did not want to return to California. By now, I had my eyes on a position with American Airlines. Once accepted into training, Miss Tate helped me study and learn the airport codes.

The woman I trained with told me I would never make it because all the students in the class were twenty years younger than myself. I knew nothing about computers and had to have constant tutoring.

Esther and Virginia were my support system, praying for me on a daily, continuous basis. Going from being a social worker to working for the airline was a huge turning point in my life; a complete career change at age forty.

Travel was something I'd wanted to pursue, ever since I was a teenager. My father was afraid of flying. He feared being in the air and believed I should fear it, too. But I did not.

Once I got my flight privileges, Dad was the last to fly. It took a lot to convince him if you really trust God you're going to trust Him on the ground or in the air.

When it's your time to go, it's not going to matter whether you're on the ground or in the air. He would not get on the plane without my 6 foot 4, almost 300-pound brother accompanying him on his very first flight. He pulled the seatbelt so tight, I thought he would strangle himself.

Once he saw the kids running up and down the aisles on that first flight, he was hooked. He'd take flights anywhere, even on prop planes after that!

God has brought me a long way, through it all. From being homeless to owning a lovely home, I've made a come-back. I am a testament to the fact that one can start from anywhere with nothing and survive – come back from anything. No matter how far down you start, you can certainly come back. I did. I came from homeless back. You can make it. There is no excuse not to do so. With God and Jesus all things are possible.

I had been saved. In Pat Boone's Church in California, I'd been saved. And there was no turning back. Regardless of what the devil had in store for me, I would be okay. *Oh, I've been tested.* Just because you accept the Lord as your Lord and Savior, there's no way you won't be tested. For you will be tested in many ways. It will not be peaches and cream. Once you accept the Lord, the devil will be out to make sure you fail. He will test you to the end. Like Job, I've been tested. Everything was taken from me.

The devil took away my job and my place to stay and pushed me down to the bottom. Staying in a shelter is something I never imagined for myself. I never thought of it as something I would have to do. At the age of forty, I had it – and then lost it – lost it all.

I used to spend. I used to have $1,000 a week available to spend. I dated a gentleman friend that had race horses. A thousand dollars a week was always available to me. So, to go down to zero was definitely something I did not relish experiencing.

From riches to rags. Everything was a cost to me. You too, will be tested.

CHAPTER 5

Compassion

How far you go in life depends on your being tender with the young, compassionate with the aged, sympathetic with the striving and tolerant of the weak and strong. Because someday in your life you will have been all of these.

— George Washington Carver

The human soul feeds on love and happiness. One must cultivate compassion to understand the suffering on the inside hidden behind a smile or a quiet manner. Self-peace and compassion begin with oneself.

I am learning how to find inner peace. It is a journey. If you don't experience the lack of love and suffering, can you truly understand? To know me, you must feel what I feel. And that is difficult because not everyone has the same experiences in life. But if you do not realize that I am suffering, you cannot help me fill my void.

The word is compassion. Lacking compassion, we will remain disconnected. What is needed, is more awareness of one another. We connect through sharing common passion. That is, a passion for life, for solitude, and for love. I do not need, nor do I love, objects and possessions. I am who I am because of the pain and because of the pleasures I have felt.

When I am caught in a negative situation, like an angry baby, I cry out. No, not an angry baby, but rather a helpless baby, crying to be picked up, to be cradled and held. I cry out to be embraced. I cry out to be embraced by positivity, by understanding, by compassion. I cannot hold the anguish inside. Silence isn't golden.

People recoil from a suffering person. They don't want to embrace the person that is in pain. It is so

> I don't have a family.
> I don't have parents.
> I don't have siblings.
> I don't have a daughter
> and I don't have my
> grandson. So, I do need
> skin on skin contact.

hard for so many, to reach out and embrace another person – skin on skin contact. People don't want that, and that's what I crave. That's what I need. That's what heals me. The touch, the human touch. There are those who say to pray, that God is with you and God never leaves you. But what about the actual skin to skin contact? We need that. Yes, I have had others pray with me and tell me God will not leave. If you believe that, you have everything you need.

34

Well, excuse me. That is not enough.

Hugs mean a lot to me. To hug someone and have them put their arms around me, to have skin on skin contact means the world to me.

We must also listen to another person. Deep listening takes time. It is work. But we need to do that. I sat with a person in pain who was suicidal. The person had no one to listen, no one to hug.

Her father was in another state far away, suffering from the tragedy of losing his wife and she felt she couldn't burden her father additionally. The conversation was not pleasant, but she needed me in that moment. I do believe that to receive compassion, one must show compassion. As human beings, we need one another.

I have been influenced by the work of Tik Nat Khan, a Vietnamese Buddhist monk who teaches people around the globe how to embrace one another as equals in a turbulent world. Khan tells us that deep listening helps relieve the suffering of a person in pain.

A troubled person will suffer less, and the suffering will continue to grow less when shown compassion, even if the things said to them are wrong. If he could, he would build a monument to world peace and brotherhood.

Let them empty their heart. Communication is important. Wait for another time to transform. For now, lessen the suffering and show compassion. Let the person know you are interested and want to understand. It is necessary to let feelings out and for them to be heard. Silence isn't golden.

Difficulties arise between friends and family and between countries. Anger arises from the energy that brews in turmoil. It is possible to find strength and faith in Buddha or Christ; the message is the same.

Show love and compassion, listen to one another, and pain will lessen. I wish more people would practice Khan's teachings. Reaching out to others is a step toward healing, for the listener and the one in need. It has worked for me.

Deep listening is something important to cultivate and practice. My best friend of forty-five years refused to listen to me. She absolutely hated listening to my stories of depression. She *refused* to listen.

She had zero compassion, zero. She did not want to hear what I had to say and therefore, my suffering continued. I found her to be so unchristian-like and so unfriendly. Compassion is everything. I have cousins who are nurses and consider themselves to be compassionate. They heal obvious, physical wounds and tend to the needs of the sick. But, I don't consider it true compassion if you can't listen to another person's suffering.

Deep listening lessens suffering. The dictionary defines compassion as, "a feeling of deep sympathy for another who is stricken by misfortune, accompanied by a strong desire to alleviate the suffering."

I don't see how listening and taking time to listen to another's pain and suffering and anxiety can be so hard. I don't care how horrible it is, you can listen. You can do so much good by taking the time to hear someone's story.

I've been told over and over again how I am soothing; I'm a good listener. I know that's in part, because I can understand.

Earlier, I talked about how, 'to know me, you must feel what I feel.' Through my own pain and circumstances in life, learning to embrace positivity and inner peace, I can listen to others to feel what they feel. I can listen deeply to their stories. I have forgotten much of my past, but I have not forgotten how to love. I have not forgotten how to show compassion, and I have not forgotten how to listen.

CHAPTER 6

Together Again

The family - that dear octopus from whose tentacles we never quite escape, nor, in our inmost hearts, ever quite wish to.

—Dodie Smith

My aged parents came to live with me in North Carolina. They needed care and I needed them close. Flying to Michigan and back, every two weeks for two years was taking a toll on my health. Together, we could establish a new routine.

My life's purpose had been to be their mouthpiece. In younger days, I felt it was my duty to be a good student, though my parents knew nothing about what I was learning in school so they were of no assistance to me for homework. I had to absorb it on my own; I was self-taught.

As time passed, I grew up and they grew old. It was time for me to take over completely. The Ten Commandments tell us, to "honor thy father and thy mother." I tried my best to fulfill my role. For twenty years, I was their caregiver. To be able to attend to their needs, I took an early retirement from the airline.

I could not count on help from relatives, many of whom lived within driving distance. Although I'd asked for help during a family reunion, I was told, "No, this is your job. This is not a family responsibility, it is a personal one."

My mother did have a sister who wrote to her frequently and learned sign language to communicate, but for the most part the family was hands-off.

People are reluctant to be involved with those whom they consider to be different, outcasts, even within the family circle. The deaf culture is an isolated one, from my parent's early days continuing to the present, I've been aware of the vicious cycle, generation to generation.

Too often, immediate family members, parents and siblings of deaf children, do not learn sign language. The children are pushed into the mainstream and the responsibility for communicating falls on the interpreter. The percentage of households where a deaf child has a family member who can sign and communicate, is unfortunately very low, less than 10%. Sad but true.

Mother had eight brothers and sisters and grew up on a tobacco farm. Because of the way her parents treated her siblings, she felt that boys were more valuable than girls. Two strikes against her; she was hearing impaired and a girl, so had little to no value.

She was sent away to the school for the deaf nine months out of the year and spent the other three months home with her family, just to help with the housework.

Mother always said she never wanted any girls, only boys. However, her boys did not care for her or favor her in return because of her handicap. Both my brothers felt my parents should not have had children, so neither would participate or volunteer to assist with my parents' care.

My relationship with my mother had been rough during my younger years. We were drawn together in a secret, silent world where unspeakable acts were protected. I know she held much anger inside. She acted out in brutal ways.

In Detroit, my mother often beat me. Thank God for Andrew Foster, the first black graduate of Gallaudet College, who was also deaf.

Foster was a friend of Mother's and lived with us between his visits to Africa, where he opened thirty-five schools for the deaf

killed in a plane crash in Rwanda while en route to Kenya in December of 1987. I believe he saved me from more beatings telling my mom to 'temper her temper' and forget what she'd learned in the south about God being a God of Punishment, and to try to learn a new way.

She tried. But, it was hard to change old ways. When Foster was not around, things were bad again. After so much time, and with her declining health, my mother and I had become closer. I know she needed me, and so I was there for her.

While living with me, Alzheimer's affected my dad and he was not himself. He was in and out of the hospital and rehab facilities.

Growing up, I'd been closer to my dad, and he was compassionate towards others. Dad worked a lot and was away from the house, unaware of much that went on there. He'd take us to visit relatives from time to time and it was good to get away from the work, punishment and beatings. In the summers, I'd spend a week with my cousins in Flint, Michigan or a week in Washington, DC with cousins.

Sometimes I'd go to North Carolina at Snow Hill for a day or two, or a week with Mother's sister in Williamston where my brother and I were like slave labor picking tobacco and using an outhouse.

We were teased because we were from the city. Mostly, those summer memories are painful.

Despite all the family reunions Mother always wanted to attend, the family was not around when my parents needed help. I am the daughter; I was there for them.

My parents had been married 61 years when Dad passed away in 1998 after a long battle with Alzheimer's.

The sins of his wife's brother, and the impact on his daughter, were never known; neither were the attacks on his wife.

My mother and I kept our secret pact intact.

The men in her life were gone. She had no sons, no husband, only me. After outliving my dad for fourteen years, Mother had to come to the realization that it was her daughter who was looking out for her and upon whom she had come to depend, the one committed to loving her unconditionally, and something clicked - **and she loved me back!**

Mother remained with me and things were going along until it became too difficult for me to care for her adequately.

She moved into a very nice retirement home in Ohio with staff that could give her what she needed. Eventually, the arthritis in her hands became too severe for her to communicate and she was not able to stay connected to her friends and family, so I did

Mom's writing for her for the years she was in Ohio.

She enjoyed getting mail so I regularly wrote letters and tried to encourage or "guilt" the recipients, and a few would write back. I visited at least every three months, sometimes more often, as a dutiful daughter.

I continued to think and act on her behalf, and believe it or not, it included writing to JDR, her rapist.

She forgave him, and he sent her regular checks. His name was on the mailing list of about thirty people to whom I wrote. She had done her own writing until the age of ninety-five.

I called the checks "guilt money" but she would never admit that's what is was. I called him out on it in Mom's later years, but he said I was a liar. He is married and I often wonder what his wife thought about these monthly checks to my mom. He was supposed to see her on her 100th birthday but that did not happen. I tried to arrange it, but it did not come to fruition. That was something on her bucket list.

Despite the difficulties of aging, she was quite content in Ohio, living to be 102 years old.

Lillie Jones, Ohio 2015 with

Trix Bruce, Hearing Impaired Interpreter / Friend

Growing Up

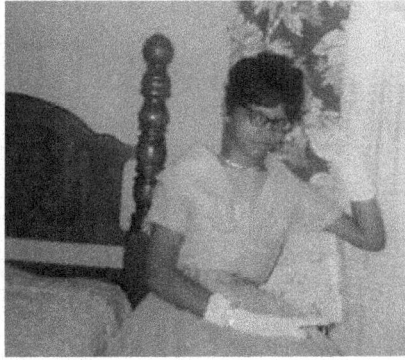

Mary Jones
Mary and Junior, upper right

Photos from the Jones Family Album

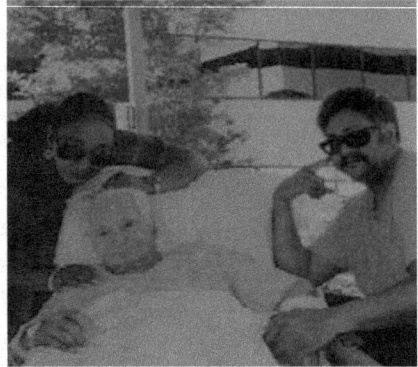

Cowgirl Mary; Lewis, Lillie, Junior, Mary & Charles
Mary & Mother Lillie; Mary & Dad Lewis & Charles

CHAPTER 7

Do Not Stand Idly By

Passion is the bridge that takes you from pain to change.

— Frida Kahlo

Do Not Stand Idly By. You do have choices. Find your own passion, do things that make you feel good about yourself. Make healing choices. Continue with things that work for you, discard those that don't. Some of the choices are:

1. Keep a 'grateful journal'
2. Meditate
3. Serve Others
4. Go to Church
5. Karma – Do good deeds so they will come back to you.

I've tried them all. Keeping a grateful journal did not work very well for me for very long. It may work for others. At the time I tried to journal, I did not find much for which to be grateful and concentrated instead on learning to know myself better.

Meditation works for me, off and on. Right now, it's working for me. Meditation in the evening can help me sleep at night, and I can relax through meditation.

Oprah Winfrey and Deepak Chopra joined together to offer 'Oprah & Deepak's 21-Day Meditation Experience' and I recorded some footage on my I-pad. Everyone knows Oprah, but you might not know Deepak Chopra. According to his website, he is a world-renowned pioneer in integrative medicine and personal transformation to help one become the person he or she was born to be. Some have called him a New Age guru. He is beloved by Oprah and the two have found a true spiritual connection which they use to help others.

If you see something that may work for you, record it, or take notes and photos to help you remember and motivate you to try it on your own.

If possible, join groups with like goals or attend sessions that cover topics you find helpful. Meditation can be an enlightening journey to help you know your inner self.

Service to others is a good one that's worked for me for many years. Going into a nursing home to spend time with the residents; playing checkers, taking them to the store, or to church with me on Sundays, and just spending time with them is so rewarding.

Too often people in nursing homes have been

thrown away or discarded by their families and don't have visitors.

Though it's been a while since I've been, I built relationships with the staff and built trust, and they would tell me who wanted a visitor and who did not. I drew close to those who wanted companionship.

My friend, Mary Sue sometimes came with me and we read the Bible and eventually went out to lunch or dinner together. That gave the residents a lot of pleasure and it gave me a lot of pleasure. So, it was a win-win.

Going to church regularly is more of a commitment. I do enjoy being around like-minded people, so it's another good thing for me to do. I went to the same church for many years and enjoyed the fellowship – great pastor. Unfortunately, the church I attend now is not as nice. It's hard to find a great church. But like all things in life, I'll keep looking until I find the one that's right for me.

Karma. For many years I have practiced 'pay it forward.' I try to sow the seeds of kindness and be a blessing. I try to 'walk the walk' and be pleasing in the eyesight of God knowing that HIS word is true. Sometimes I do have anger issues with God wondering when this karma is going to be returned. I hear it all the time, "what goes around, comes around."

I fed the entire floor of residents at the nursing home in my dad's rehab unit for a year. I volunteered at the nursing homes in my area for ten years. I am constantly showing compassion to others whenever and wherever I can.

At the Dollar Store when the person in front of me wants to put things back because they don't have the money for their order, I pay it for them. At a drive-through restaurant, I've handed the cashier money for the car behind me. At a gas station, anywhere I can do something to bring a little bit of joy to someone's life, friend or stranger, I do it.

It's always good to be able to do something for someone else, anonymously and unconditionally. It gives you pleasure. It's really a good feeling. Those you help, will never know who you are.

Maybe it comes back around to me, I don't know. If it does, I consider that to be karma.

Don't sit idly by when you are going through troubled times. These things will help you heal. They truly, truly will help you heal and will take your mind off those things with which you are dealing. I don't know how God does it, but through these methods He will help you grow and heal.

Paying it forward has come full circle in the preparation for publishing the book you are now reading. A few years ago, I met a woman named Cornelia McDonald shopping in a local thrift store, *Pass It On,* run by a woman named Laura Hilton for the INTERACT organization for battered women. Cornelia had written a book and I was delighted to help her promote it.

In fact, Cornelia was the reason I decided to write a book and I looked forward to her helping me in penning my story. However, her life was cut short and God took her home.

We had been able, during our friendship, to make some wonderful connections. Cornelia and I flew to Chicago to promote her book with Zelda Robinson, a motivational speaker and fitness/wellness coach. The relationship between Cornelia and Zelda blossomed so much that Zelda had invited Cornelia back for a second appearance. All were thrilled!

I also sent Cornelia to Los Angeles on my airline pass to find an agent for her book - and she did. Her cancer was in remission and she was ecstatic! Cornelia was on Cloud 9 and I so badly wanted her book to take off. I surprised Cornelia with a limo for her book signing in Raleigh and gave her the VIP treatment!

She introduced me to a talented artist named Pinkie Strother at an art showing. Cornelia had been able to find someone in Los Angeles to assist Pinkie in gaining International recognition for her art work.

My book was on hold, but I was okay with that. Cornelia's cancer returned and unfortunately, she and I were never able to collaborate on my book.

So, the idea went back into the drawer for almost a year until I joined my writer's group and was encouraged by my fellow writers to complete the manuscript.

To close the circle, Pinkie continued the karma by 'paying it forward' and designed the beautiful cover for this book because she knew all that I had done for Cornelia.

My heart is heavy with all the stories I have heard over the years as an interpreter from the girls and boys attending schools for the deaf. These are children who are not main-streamed, but are housed in the schools 24/7 like my parents. I have spoken to fellow interpreters about it and they conclude that it is a 90% true rate with the children, boys and girls – they have heard the same stories.

Kids are molested in those schools and the incidents are swept under the rug. These children are at the mercy of those in charge. They truly do not have a voice. I have had female clients so traumatized that now, as deaf adults, they do not wear dresses, because they do not want to be easily accessible. Did their parents know? Who knows? Do you know? It's a matter of, "If you stand idly by, you are part of the problem and not a part of the solution."

In the words of Maya Angelou, "If you know better, you should do better. If you do not, then I do not want to be you, come Judgement Day!" When you see something – you do something. I have crossed the line many a time to assist someone that needed my help and my conscience is clear. I may have missed a paycheck here and there as a result, but one cannot put a price on being able to sleep at night. I sleep with a clear conscience.

Do not stand idly by. You may not see immediate results from the good you do for others, but God is keeping track. When it's your turn, you'll be rewarded. The important thing is to get out and do things that make you feel good about yourself and that bring good to others. You must jump in and start the cycle.

CHAPTER 8

Best Buds

We delight in the beauty of the butterfly, but rarely admit the changes it has gone through to achieve that beauty.

— Maya Angelou

At sixteen I was married, at seventeen, a mother of a baby girl, my only child.

The marriage ended when I was twenty-one. Like most failed marriages when the partners are children themselves, there was much we did not know. The biggest thing, of course, was not knowing how to trust and nurture one another. We did a terrible job of trying to be adults. I never married again. If I ever do, it will be forever.

Soon after the divorce, I became romantically involved with a man I was sure would give me everything I needed. Remember the man with the race horses and the unlimited spending budget? That was Raymond. He was flashy and flirtatious, and generous to me. I guess I was impressed with his manners and money.

One Christmas he'd promised me a new car. I picked out the one I wanted, a triple black Monte Carlo, a beautiful vehicle, and one I felt would make me feel special to drive. Raymond told the dealer to load it up with whatever I asked for, and he boasted that he'd be paying cash. Money was no object if I was happy. The car had to be ordered with all the upgrades and features I wanted.

The day the call came from the dealership that the car had arrived, I was excited! I couldn't wait to go and pick it up. At last, something good after so much trauma.

My little daughter pleaded with me to take her along, but I said it was better for her to stay home with a friend and despite her crying to go, I didn't give in. I am so thankful for that decision.

When we arrived, only the salesman was present. "Where is everyone?" I asked curiously, looking around at the empty showroom.

"Christmas party", he replied. "Everyone left early for a Christmas party."

As we began to fill out the paper work, two men flashing guns burst into the room and said the deal was off! There would be no car. The cash was theirs and we'd be coming with them back across town where we lived, as though the whole thing never happened. No car and no deal and we never came there. In fact, they'd just take us back and kill us.

First, they demanded that Raymond remove his rings and fancy watch and give those items to them. They looked at my ring but didn't want it. These were picky robbers.

The ride across town was terrifying! I sat in the front with the barrel of a gun in my waist. Raymond was in the back seat with a gun pointed at him.

I started to pray out loud begging God to hear my pleas and get us out of the situation.

"Please, God, don't let us die!" Over and over I called out in prayer.

"Shut up!" the driver screamed. "I'm sick of hearing you pray to God. Shut up or I'll have to kill you right now!"

I prayed in silence.

Raymond yelled from the back seat! "Jump out! Jump out! I'm going to jump!"

I yelled back, "Are you kidding? I'm not jumping out of a moving car!"

"Then jump out when we stop at a light! I'm

jumping!" he screamed.

The car stopped at a light and miraculously, the kidnappers let us go. One of them threw the keys to our car in the bushes and they took off.

Raymond was determined to return to the dealership because during the robbery, he'd tossed one of his rings under a desk and he wanted it back.

The building was closed when we arrived. Raymond called the police who opened the building and took our report.

The ring under the desk was proof of the story and gave us the credibility needed for the officers to pursue the criminals.

Of course, you have realized by now, that the salesman was part of the plot and set the whole thing up. Such a tangled, terrifying event.

In the trial that followed a year later, all were convicted. Raymond got his money, I got my car.

I left Detroit and Raymond after my brother was killed in 1976. I could not stay any longer.

I packed up and took my daughter to California to start again.

Since that time, I have started again and again

and again.

I ask God for a husband. I am the QUEEN of online dating and have been on more than eighty online dates. I stopped counting after eighty. Let me tell you about one of the guys from one of these *great* dates – we became engaged. I thought to myself, *"Oh, my God, no other man is ever going to ask me to marry him, so I'd better say yes!"*

A friend in Los Angeles threw me an engagement party. When she met the man, I'll call him Frank, she asked,

"Mary, what were you thinking?"

I said I was desperate! Frank was ten years younger than me. I just wanted to be married more than anything in this world. God tells us in the first Book of the Bible, that Adam should have a companion, so why shouldn't I?

I had a proposal. I had a ring. We got the license. My pastor counseled us. I was going to make this work.

But there were plenty of red flags! Frank was making $1,000 a week and was retired! From what, I did not know. He wouldn't tell me!

He had no sisters, no brothers, no parents, no job.

We flew to Las Vegas. We flew to Ohio to see my mom. The pastor told him, the therapist told him, I told him, "There will not be any, 'I Do' until Mary knows how you come by the money you have." He wrote me a check for $15,000 and said he'd tell me AFTER I'd said, 'I Do.' I told him it would not work like that.

If he could not trust me, I could not marry him.

He was a country bumpkin who'd never flown before he met me. When in the Garment District in Los Angeles, he bought every name-brand suit he could carry. We had to buy luggage just for his suits. When we were in Las Vegas, he was shocked that prostitutes were legal. He wanted to order one!

He was just in awe, almost like the time my mom stayed out all night with the drug dealers because she wanted to see what it was really like rather than just seeing it on television.

I have prayed and prayed...God...where are the people? Where are the ones with 'skin on' – the encouragers? The supporters? You didn't assign them to me at birth. I don't have them as an extended family, no village around me. I have to parent myself and then learn to re-parent myself.

I had been sowing the seeds along the way, and along came Sasha.

I asked for a two-legged companion and God sent a four-legged one. I hadn't had a dog in thirty years. "No more dogs!" I'd always said. But when a lady could no longer care for Sasha, I agreed to take her in, I stepped up and said, "I'll take the dog."

I felt it was more of a rescue situation. This is not a working dog, like others I've had. This is a loving dog, a lap dog. We have a bond, Sasha and I, with a love unlike any other. She can sleep in my bed. Me and Sasha! Best Buds! Sasha rescued me and gave me love.

So, she's here with me and I accept Sasha as my loving companion while I still wait for God to deliver someone with "SKIN ON." Still praying for **THE ONE**!

You too, may be seduced by the glitter of gold and the smooth talk of a manipulator. Remember, that you are worthy of true love and deserve the best. Do not give into temptation or settle for something that is not going to fulfill your deepest needs for heartfelt affection. You will be tested and like Job, you must have patience.

Eckhart Tolle, a German-born spiritual healer and teacher tells us,

"Boredom, anger, sadness, or fear are not yours, not personal. They are conditions of the human mind. They come and go. Nothing that comes and goes is you. The past has no power over the present moment. Some changes look negative on the surface, but you will soon realize that space is being created in your life for something new to emerge. The primary cause of unhappiness is never the situation but your thoughts about it."

When you are feeling down, be careful not to fill the space Eckhart speaks of, with more negativity. Let the new conditions that emerge be positive and fulfilling. Discard those that do not serve your purpose of healing.

CHAPTER 9

A Plan to Heal

"For I know the plans I have for you," declares the Lord. "Plans to prosper you and not to harm you, plans to give you hope and a future."

— *Jeremiah 29: 11* (NIV)

Life's full of challenges and moments of joy.

I am ready for the next chapter. God opened my eyes to Oprah and Dr. Phil and the way to healing through choices. So next time I hear someone ask, "How's it working for you?" I will answer, "It's working well, my friend".

I am making better choices. It's a journey to be sure. I put one foot in front of the other and go on.

I have struggled most of my life with weight issues. I keep losing weight and it keeps finding me. There was a time when I was obese. I've lost eighty pounds and like many, have covered my pain with bad choices. I have been a size 8 for about six years now, which is the smallest I've been in probably twenty years. Up and down that rollercoaster of weight. It's something one does to cover up the pain. It's a choice that we make a lot.

People that have been molested and abused cover up with weight and food.

With an eating disorder and food issues for the last six years, I've had to make new choices. I've been able to hold my weight down and my size to an 8 or 10 which is perfect for me. I love it and I love the size I am. Together with exercise, it's something that can be done by making the right choices.

Coping mechanisms can take many forms. Looking for ways to close off the past and cover the wounds with a band aid, give immediate relief, but don't get at the root of the wound. As I mentioned earlier, I have been asked by many therapists,

"Why are you depressed today?

What's holding you down, now?"

Even professionals cannot always help you unburden yourself from the tormenting past.

There are so many connections from my childhood that haunt me to this day. After all the chores and household duties thrust upon me, it was liberating to hire my first housekeeper as soon as I could afford to when I lived in Los Angeles. I still have a housekeeper today. As a young girl, I ironed so many sheets and towels and underwear and my dad's work clothes. I don't iron anything to this day. All the monotonous meals, all the 'cabbage Mondays' and 'string bean Wednesdays' – yuck to both!

I have had more than my share of turmoil and tribulation in the past six decades. I have been dealt a hard blow, again and again, kicked to the ground by life. I have had to stand up and start over and over and over.

Please believe me, you cannot heal on your own. I have tried to work through lingering issues on my own. Yes, I too, want to know why I am depressed today or what's holding me down now. But, I believe the answers lie somewhere in the ignominies of my disjointed early years. Digging through like a miner looking for treasure, I keep hoping to spot a glimmer of gold to brighten my way.

As long as I struggle with old wounds, I am stymied in taking steps toward my future life. I know I must first learn to love myself. I must know I am worthy of the love. I must be able to rid myself of the guilt and the shame and all the problems I carry like an albatross around my neck. I am haunted by thoughts of molestation, of lying helpless in my crib and waiting for the next attack, of my mother in the dark, behind closed doors being raped by that boxer, feeling afraid and unable to do anything about it, of the endless police reports, and the secrets. I had no voice as a child and then I became the voice of my mother, but still the assaults would not stop.

People without a voice rely on others to be an interpreter. For young people who cannot speak, who are mute, an interpreter is how they convey their voices to the world. The circle is small. Many who rely on others to interpret for them, have no one else to talk to. Even at home, they are isolated. And all too often, the most vulnerable are the easiest targets.

Children are molested by family members. It is so terribly sad, but I know this to be true. Girls like me, from a young age of two or three, not able to talk about what's happening, not supported by their families or even abandoned by those who are supposed to love and protect them, suffer in silence.

If one does not have a childhood and has not been able to deal with the wounds of abuse; if she is not loved by her family, and has ended up in a horrible situation as an adult, how then can she look in the mirror and say, "I love you"? How do you begin this process of loving yourself? It is a journey and I have begun.

CHAPTER 10

Road to the Future

My dear, In the midst of hate, I found there was, within me, an invincible love. In the midst of tears, I found there was, within me, an invincible smile. In the midst of chaos, I found there was, within me, an invincible calm. I realized through all, that, in the midst of winter, I found there was, within me, an invincible summer. And that makes me happy. For it says that no matter how hard the world pushes against me, within me, there's something stronger – something better, pushing right back.

— Albert Camus

Through the years I think I've had a lot of anger issues. I *know* I've had lots, really. Not finding any joy in my life – leaving Christianity to become a Muslim and struggling to know myself and find my own way.

My mother would tell me that God was about punishment, not about love. So, I went as far away from Christianity as I could possibly go without becoming an atheist. I was after all, craving something, craving love. I became acquainted with Islam and the Koran. I learned about the Islam religion and Arabic, far from Christianity.

People ask how I returned to Christianity after studying Islam and the Koran for so many years. Well, I did not even have a Bible in my home and lived a quiet life learning Arabic with my friends. Then, things started to happen that were completely unexplainable. Living in Los Angeles, earthquakes were normal, *but not mine.* Mine happened regularly! I had fiery darts that would leave me hovering in the bathroom corner. Furniture moved! Noises on the roof that only I could hear! Drawings appeared on my wall and I had photographers come and take pictures, but the photos would not develop.

I'd ask the neighbor in the adjoining townhouse if she could see or hear what I was seeing and hearing? Her reply was always the same.

"No! You are the only one being attacked." She'd repeat the words, "In the name of Jesus, I demand you leave" and 'instantly' it would stop!

My friends told me to leave and move out. I replied, "Why? It's something that follows me, and there is no escape." Finally, my neighbor asked me if I had a Bible. I said, "No." She said, "Well you are in a battle and I urge you to get one!" I did.

I began reading the Bible and studying the passages. After a nine-month battle that I equate to the conversion of Saul to Paul on the road to Damascus, Jesus set out to prove to me that HE is the son of God! And by golly, He did! I was baptized in Pat Boone's 'Church on the Way' and never looked back!

Leaving Detroit. Moving to California. After my baby brother was murdered. Not discovering my voice. Not knowing how to use my voice, give credence to the voice. The voice of the child. The child in the crib that was molested by my mother's brother.

My own Uncle Claude was the one-armed man who molested me from the age of two to possibly age eight or nine when we moved from Hendricks Street to Tuxedo Street, from the east side of Detroit to the west side. I don't remember any more for some reason. And then, that was when my mother rented the room out to JDR who began to rape her.

I don't remember Uncle Claude coming around anymore. Maybe he passed away or became ill. I don't remember the reason why. I was always instructed not to tell my father. I do remember that. I couldn't tell my father about the rape of my mother by the tenant. No talking about it – was always swept under the rug. Sweep it under the rug and not talk about it, so I didn't.

When my daughter was molested I did not have the mentality of *not* discussing it with her. My best friend chose not to believe her, but I knew the truth. I was the only one who believed her; that she'd been molested. My friend's live-in boyfriend admitted to me that he did molest her. His admission was over the phone and he said he would never admit it outside of that phone conversation.

I had my daughter hypnotized so that my friend would know too. Despite all the confirmation, she continued to deny the reality.

I had a lot of guilt in this horrific situation because I felt like it happened on my watch. *How could I let this happen to my daughter?*

I lost my daughter and I lost my best friend. My daughter and I are estranged and haven't seen one another for many years. She does not want to have anything to do with me and withholds my grandson from my life.

I know my daughter suffers from a phenomenon called, 'parent alienation'. First recognized by the psychological community as occurring during divorce when a child sides with one parent and cuts emotional ties with the other, it is now known to extend to other circumstances and to carry into adult parent-child relationships, or lack thereof.

Sometimes the basis is irrational, sometimes legitimate. In any case, the child will have no guilt for the feelings and no concern for the alienated parent.

My best friend and I have ended our friendship after forty-five years. I don't know if it's completely due to the incident with my daughter, but maybe that's the main reason. I don't mind the breakup so much.

I just don't have the will to fight for the friendship. She really didn't believe that her boyfriend did anything to my daughter because she felt if he lived in the house, *why would he not molest her daughter?* But I knew from what my daughter said and from his admission that it did occur. I don't think to this day that my friend believes that it happened.

> *To everything there is a season, and a time for every purpose under the heaven; a time to be born, and a time to die; a time to plant, and a time to pluck up that which is planted; a time to kill, and a time to heal; a time to break down, and a time to build up; a time to weep, and a time to laugh; a time to mourn, and a time to dance; a time to cast away stones, and a time to*

gather stones together; a time to embrace, a time to refrain from embracing; a time to get, a time to lose; a time to keep, and a time to cast away; a time to reap, and a time to sow; a time to keep silence, and a time to speak; a time to love, and a time to hate; a time of war, and a time of peace. Ecclesiastes 3: 1-8 (KJV)

I had called and asked for an 'eye to eye' meeting to see if we could work out our differences. The answer from my friend was, "No!" So, I felt God was uprooting and removing this person due to the seasonal change. Forty-five years is a long-term investment, but when the time was up, I did not fight it. Now, was the time to refrain from embracing. I sleep well, and my heart is at peace.

I know the road to my future begins with the first step I take. Making notes about positive ways to help me find the way, are essential. They can be mental notes or can be written down and read over from time to time.

These are take-aways from a lifetime of trials, of being tested. Some may be of help to you, too.

One: Speak up! And Speak out! Make a commitment to yourself – No more secrets – No more sweeping it under the rug.

Two: Talk it out with someone you trust or write it out. You can keep a journal or just record thoughts and feelings. The main thing is to do it!

Three: Remind yourself, "I am free to love intentionally." You choose who to love and for what reasons, but for the right reasons. Make good choices!

Four: Remind yourself often, "I am not alone." And, "I have a voice!"

Oprah and Deepak tell us that forming a lasting habit takes repetition. You must keep practicing. It takes 21 days to make a habit. I was told by a doctor that doing something you hate will not stick.

Whether its meditation or walking or exercise you hate doing, find a way to make it a good habit. That might mean just doing it for five minutes a day. You don't have to get on a treadmill; put on a record and dance! Five minutes will turn into ten, and ten into twenty. Soon you will form a habit.

By following my doctor's advice, I was able to forget about a treadmill and get outside and walk; up to the church and back, then past the church, then before I knew it, three miles and then ten years had become a lifelong habit.

By writing my story and sharing with those who read it, my voice is going to be heard. Finally. Being heard. Then I can file it away.

Possibly the well will break open and I can find some joy. I feel I have it coming. The joy and love that I have missed all these years, from the age of two until now.

Here I am in my 60's. For you, my audience, I say to you, find help to lead you to joy and love before you get to this point. Hopefully, you can identify with what I've relayed.

Looking for unconditional love has been difficult. I know that I must first be able to look in the mirror, and say, "I love you." Until that day, I cannot fulfil the things on my bucket list. But I won't stop taking steps in a positive direction.

This is a journey. Even the longest journey, begins with a single step. Obstacles will slow you down, you will have setbacks and falls. On my journey, I am constantly ambushed by my memories. Everyday life is full of triggers to slow my progress along this road. Smells, sounds, places, television dramas, real life dramas, songs and images, are there to remind me. You too, will get knocked down, but get back up and continue.

If you don't think you have the support you need, or the voice to speak out, know that you do. You have the voice. Speak up! Speak out! And find an avenue to lead you to the life you deserve.

Seek other options. Because, certainly, there is a path to healing. This is my path to healing and I am on my way. A path is available to you.

Do not wait any longer, because indeed, keeping it silent and sweeping it under the rug is not the answer. Steve Harvey says, "Jump off that cliff and get started!"

So, let's take that jump. Start by opening up your mouth and giving it a voice. Let's start on that path to joy, love and healing, because all those paths are open.

CHAPTER 11

Worldly Reminders

Sometimes memories sneak out of my eyes and roll down my cheeks.

— *Unknown*

I watch a lot of television. Sometimes I have it on without the sound, just for company, to fill the room so I'm not alone. Other times, I find myself absorbed in the stories portrayed by actors on the screen. Too many times, images resting precariously on the edge of my memory take over and carry me back to a dark place, triggered by something said or done by the fictional characters I'm watching.

My memories are not fiction, they are real. While writing notes for this book, I was watching an episode of "Law and Order, Special Victims Unit" in which a rape victim is asking Mariska Hargitay if she knows what it feels like to have her legs ripped open. Does she understand what it feels like to be raped? And suddenly, it's a flashback for me. I'm back in my crib.

Well in a crib, your legs are not forced open. A

baby, a child doesn't know how to resist. The molester knows he doesn't have to force your legs open. They don't have to be forced because they are already pliable. Babies are 'willing participants' because they don't know any better. The child is the most pliable subject and the most pliable victim. To pick on somebody that young, the youngest victim, is so horribly wrong.

That "Law and Order: Special Victims Unit" episode was really about exposing the males who are doing things to the youngest population, babies and children, who don't even have the voice to say, "No!"

Because of position or authority, men could get away with abusing their victims. A child who is unsupported and unprotected can easily become a victim. A family member, a friend, or a neighbor who is in contact with the young person on a regular basis can become the abuser.

I also watched an awful series on the Menendez brothers killing their parents. Those episodes were also mindful of remembrances of the same thing. Is the ending more atrocious because they were so abused by their parents that they were driven to kill them? It was just a dreadful end to the disturbing childhood they had.

But certainly, I did identify with some of their abuse as well. There were at least seven episodes, but I stopped watching after the first two. I couldn't watch anymore.

Then I separated myself from them for quite a while. I don't even remember how old it is, and usually I don't do that. I usually don't start a miniseries and stop. They must have been so painful I couldn't watch them anymore.

In fact, I had to do a review on them and I gave a poor review. When, I shouldn't have because they turned out to be well done. If I didn't like it, I should have just deleted it, but I couldn't, and still I could not bear to watch it until later. I didn't want to revisit those wounds.

I heard on Jimmy Kimmel's late-night show - a guest talked about a Thanksgiving prank saying "Happy Thanksgiving" to everybody except females because if you were a female, you had nothing for which to be thankful. All the shows were about men being fired from their jobs for molesting somebody either presently or ten years ago or forty years ago.

So many have been on the news for being relieved of their position or resigning in advance of becoming fired. For several weeks, it was daily news. Somebody else has gotten fired.

So, that's why the joke was - that if you were a female you identified with one of those females in some capacity. So, "Happy Thanksgiving" was not going to be if you were a female in any shape or form. Somebody had probably done something to you if you are a female and you've nothing for which to be thankful. That was the comedic joke being told.

There is a group of the population, namely girls who were molested as babies and children, who are coming forward now. This is the segment I'm in.

There are also women speaking out about having been sexually assaulted or molested by men who were their bosses. Men are being exposed for past wrongdoings and are being fired. They are in the news every day. I believe this is my window of opportunity to give the most press for all groups.

I should be able to get a better audience while everybody's got a heightened awareness for this subject. I want to garner attention for these women and their plight, their struggles and their desire to find healing.

I've also read a lot of books and articles to assist my journey forward. One that I recommend highly, is "The Purpose Driven Life" with the subtitle, "What on Earth Am I Here For?" - by Rick Warren.

Rather than looking for solutions within oneself, the author tells us we must look to God. Everything comes from Him.

If you haven't listened to Deepak Chopra on meditation, try that. Find the place to begin your healing that works for you. Deepak and his daughter, Mallika, teach how to live with intention by focusing on purpose and putting an end to the suffering. I know God only gives us enough grace for one day, so that's a perfect way to live your life, one day at a time.

Why worry about tomorrow, since tomorrow is not promised? Live today with your best intentions and enough light to share with someone else. We have to love one another. That is a direct quote from God in my eyesight. *"Love one another."*

If we could love one another, we'd certainly be doing a better job of making peace in the world.

CHAPTER 12

Let There Be Light

You are always a valuable, worthwhile human being – not because anybody says so, not because you're successful, not because you make a lot of money – but because you decide to believe it and for no other reason.

— *Wayne Dyer*

In my prayers I ask God to bless me and to be a blessing to someone else during the course of that day. If I can offer a smile to somebody to brighten their day, I have given what I have to offer. Certainly, we can do that for one another. If I can bless another by doing that, I will have shared my love.

I am a certified Ambassador for Peace through a world organization by that name. Regardless of one's religious beliefs, being a Muslim or a Jew or whatever your religion, we are all more alike than different. Religion was created for man. God and Christ were here before religion. Christ was not made for religion. So, we have got to stop trying to say, "this religion is right, and that religion is wrong." It is up to God. We cannot be judging one another. That is not our job. As we come to the close of this book, remember to live your life with grace and peace and love. Practice grace for one day and learn to meditate, try to live intentionally, and put one foot in front of the other.

This is not an easy course and there will be setbacks and falls along the way. Just as I was taking a turn and heading in a positive direction, about a year ago, I had a monumental setback.

"What, you might ask, could cause a monumental setback after a life of turbulence?"

Sasha and I were out for my routine exercise walk when I was knocked down by a truck! I suffered intense trauma including a head injury and a concussion that affected my memory even more than before the accident. She was small enough to be able to escape under the wheels.

Yes, that happened to me. And I am still here. I am back on my feet and putting one foot forward and then the other. I am still trying to live my life with intention.

I hope that you can live yours with intention, be a blessing to someone else and serve others. Let's try doing something to be a blessing to someone else. Know that you are worthy of love and you can heal. The reason I keep trying, is "faith"—faith that God has promised in Psalms 37: 4. He will give me the desires of my heart. HE keeps HIS word. So far, I don't have them. I don't have the man and I don't have the fruits of my labor and that "season of rest".

Sarah was age 90 before she got her answer in the Bible. Job got thirty-eight chapters of harshness. So, I have to believe that in due season mine is coming.

I have tried to use my voice and at times, it was not heard. I tried for nine years to refinance my house. I did not quit. The tenth year, I finally got it done! Although I could not avoid bankruptcy, Faith and God brought me through a harsh time. Sometimes you will use your voice and be ignored. Store clerks and friends and powerful people may ignore you; they have me.

Even when you are not heard, you still have to go on. Even though life seems unfair and it truly is not fair in lots of situations, you fall down, but get back up again. I was not quiet during these times, not at all! I used my voice and kept crying out until it was heard!

Behind the dark door, shines a ray of light. Open the door wide and shine the light on you. Don't ever give up. Don't ever stop speaking out!

You do have a voice. Silence isn't golden.

God's blessings to each and every one who hears this message. God Bless.

RESOURCES

- "A New Earth" Eckhart Tolle
- Andrew Foster: Read more at sites such as, www.deafis.org/culture/celebrities/foster.php www.mydeafchild.org/resources

  www.deafwebsites.com/hearing-impaired-resources.html

  www.deafchildren.org
- www3.gallaudet.edu (they recommended the Nursing Home for the Deaf where my mom was a resident (from age 95-102) in Columbus Ohio (Columbus Colony for aged Deaf Residents
- www.trixbruce.com (Picture with my Mom) Great Interpreter and Instructor who went out of her way to meet my mom)
- www.marleematlinsite.com/people/marlee-matlin.html (Children of a Lesser God) A favorite Actress who also is in *Switched at Birth*
- MeToo. Join the movement to support survivors and end sexual violence. https://metoomvmt.org/
- Women's foundation launches fund to support MeToo movement https://www.apnews.com/c07113f1a73047a589eed d1ef936fecb
- WATCH: Tarana Burke On How to Support the #MeToo Movement ...

https://www.colorlines.com/articles/watch-tarana-burke-how-support-metoo-movement

- Your Role in Preventing Sexual Assault | RAINN
https://www.rainn.org/articles/your-role-preventing-sexual-assault
- It's On Us to stop sexual assault
https://www.itsonus.org/
- If you've experienced sexual assault and need crisis support, **call National Sexual Assault Hotline at 1-800-656-HOPE (4673).**
- 100 Things You Can Do to Prevent Sexual Assault - UC Davis CARE
https://care.ucdavis.edu/docs/100thingsSa.pdf
- www.interactofwake.org Interact is the only provider of domestic violence and sexual assault services in Wake Co., NC- saving lives, rebuilding lives and securing safer futures for individuals and families in our community.

I Will Use My Voice!

MY EMERGENCY HELP LINES:

IMMEDIATE EMERGENCY - DIAL 911

- DOMESTIC VIOLENCE _____
- SEXUAL ABUSE _____
- COUNSELING _____
- FRIEND OR NEIGHBOR_____
- SHELTER _____

OTHER_____

OTHER _____

SPECIAL ACKNOWLEDGEMENTS

To Vickie Wilson, whom I met at an Art Fair and while discussing my book idea, Vickie told me about her book club, offering to drive me to a meeting to help get this book started. Pure compassion - so rare these days. So, there is karma for seeds sown that come back - you never know from whom or in what form. Vickie encouraged and supported me every step of the way. Vickie is a great artist, an angel and a blessing, and a wonderful Sister in Christ.

To Carol Clark, whom I happened to meet in the nail salon; the latest angel God has assigned to me. She has two daughters and grandchildren galore – enough to share with me! I especially need them during holidays, the loneliest times without family. Carol has added her editing talent to assist with my book.

To my niece, Cara Dye and her boys, Kris and Kam who know how hard the holidays are for me being alone and never miss a beat sending cards and presents to make sure I feel special and am not forgotten. Cara, who lost her father (my brother), then her mother, then her brother, finds time to remember me. Cara has unlimited compassion and the biggest heart I know! We are like mother and daughter.

To Bishop Bola Adeoti, who was instrumental in assisting me while caring for my dad throughout his illness and helping me grieve his death. Over the years, my rock steady friend through trials and tribulations with my mom. Bishop is still there for me, even when a handyman is nowhere to be found to repair a toilet.

To Juanita Lee, a real sister in Christ, who doesn't just talk the talk, she walks the walk. For the past ten years, one of the few looking out for me and finding support when problems fall on my doorstep, from helping with my taxes to finding someone to mow my grass. She is phenomenal in more ways than I can count!

To Tom Campion, a dear friend from American Airlines, who helped me relocate my parents from Michigan to North Carolina, and who learned to sign, just enough to give me respite, and assist me with family matters when my own family would not. At the passing of my mother, Tom came through in a big way and I thank God for him. We are still the best of friends even though he lives in Texas with his wonderful family.

To Ellen Doak (Sasha's other mother) and my friend! I would never have known I could care for another dog like I care for Sasha and then to be blessed with Ellen who loves her just as much as I do. It gives me so much relief knowing I can leave Sasha with someone who loves her, when I travel or go anywhere. She is such a blessing. God surely placed us together!

To Gloria Holder, another African-American interpreter with whom I can identify in this crazy racially charged world still prevalent within the interpreting community. It's so good to be able to communicate and navigate in an environment that still doesn't make sense. My black mother and her white roommate, and only one is allowed an interpreter? Rules that apply to some, not others, without rationale. She understands; a great friend and of course we are in the minority!

To Cousin Daisy Rae, who came to stay with me during my sinus surgery two years ago. Finally, a relative stepped up. Not just any relative – one who had a cousin CB, who was deaf and mute, and a mom with Alzheimer's. Having her with me to care about me was a new feeling. A great feeling and I loved it! We are the same age and grew up semi-together. Dad would drive us to Snow Hill every summer to her home to spend time with her family. They all know sign language!

I depended on T.V. as my companion for a lot and as my entertainment during a lot of dry spells in my life. So, I want to give thanks,

To Chris Rock and Steve Harvey - for laughter is a great medicine;

To Oprah Winfrey, as a great source of encouragement and inspiration;

To Tyler Perry, whose story parallels mine and whose Medea Plays are "da bomb" - I love his "Haves and Have Nots" weekly dramas to take my mind off my own troubles, and "Queen Sugar," also;

To Jimmy Kimmel, whose late-night comedy gives me a nice smile to end my day;

To Trevah Noah, whose great sense of humor adds to more laughter at night;

To Tiffany Haddish, who is my hero from "Girls Trip" and for our love of *Groupons*!

And finally, to "Law and Order: SVU," my night time sleep partner, who I go to sleep with every night!

Me and my four-legged sleep partner, Sasha

ABOUT THE AUTHOR

Mary Shelton lives and works in Fuquay-Varina, North Carolina having resided in the area for nearly three decades. She has served on the Board of Directors of the Optimist Club, is a member of the Fuquay-Varina Writers Guild, and is a certified Ambassador for Peace. Mary was born and raised in Detroit, Michigan to hearing-impaired parents and worked as a Social Worker in Michigan and California. After a family tragedy, she moved to California in 1976 where she continued her career in Social Work and taught American Sign Language at California State University at Northridge. ASL is Mary's first language.

After settling in North Carolina in 1989, she began a career with American Airlines, taking early retirement after 15 years to care for her aging parents in her home. She became an Interpreter for the Deaf. More than a job, it was a commitment to a voiceless community; a commitment she continues to this day.

Mary has a passion for the hearing-impaired and their treatment both in and out of institutions. This is her first book chronicling her life living with parents who could not hear and did not speak along with the unkind treatment they suffered because of their disabilities. Mary, too was caught in the family cycle. Her book tells about the sexual abuse she endured at the hands of a relative and how it has impacted her life. She encourages all who suffer any kind of abuse to speak out until someone listens and helps. Silence indeed, is Not Golden!

Journal Notes

Journal Notes

Journal Notes

Journal Notes

Journal Notes

Journal Notes

Journal Notes

Journal Notes

Journal Notes

Journal Notes

Journal Notes

Journal Notes

Journal Notes

Journal Notes

Journal Notes

Journal Notes

Journal Notes

Journal Notes

Journal Notes

Journal Notes

Journal Notes

Journal Notes

Journal Notes

Journal Notes

Journal Notes

Journal Notes

Journal Notes

Journal Notes

Journal Notes

Journal Notes

Journal Notes

Journal Notes

Journal Notes

Journal Notes

Journal Notes

Journal Notes

Journal Notes

Journal Notes

Journal Notes

Journal Notes

Author

authormaryshelton@gmail.com
FB:@Godisiam

Never Give Up!

Never Forget- You Have A Voice!

www.ingramcontent.com/pod-product-compliance
Lightning Source LLC
Chambersburg PA
CBHW071130090426
42736CB00012B/2073